This Planner Belongs To:

A Look At My Assets & Liabilities

YEARLY FINANCIAL Goals

THIS YEAR *my primary goals are*

JAN

FEB

MAR

APR

MAY

JUN

JUL

AUG

SEP

OCT

NOV

DEC

BALANCE Sheet

DATE: **FINANCIALS**

CREDIT SCORE: LIABILITIES: ASSETS:

NET WORTH:

ASSETS	AMOUNT	LIABILITIES	AMOUNT
CASH		**DEBTS**	
SUBTOTAL:		SUBTOTAL:	
INVESTMENTS		**LOANS**	
SUBTOTAL:		SUBTOTAL:	
REAL ESTATE		**MORTGAGE**	
SUBTOTAL:		SUBTOTAL:	
OTHER		**OTHER**	
SUBTOTAL:		SUBTOTAL:	

DEBT REPAYMENT *Plan*

ACCOUNT:　　　　　　　　　　　　　　　　**WEBSITE URL:**

PRIORITY#

CREDIT TYPE:　　　　　　　　　　USERNAME:　　　　　　　PASSWORD:

CREDIT LIMIT:

　　　　　　　　　　　　　　　　　STARTING BALANCE:

GOAL PAYOFF DATE

　　　　　　　　　　　　　　INTEREST ACCRUED:　　　　DUE DATE:

PAYMENT DATE　　　　　**PAYMENT AMOUNT**　　　　**CURRENT BALANCE**

DEBT REPAYMENT *Plan*

ACCOUNT: **WEBSITE URL:**

PRIORITY#

COMPANY: USERNAME: PASSWORD:

CREDIT TYPE:

CREDIT LIMIT: **STARTING BALANCE:**

GOAL PAYOFF DATE

INTEREST ACCRUED: DUE DATE:

PAYMENT DATE **PAYMENT AMOUNT** **CURRENT BALANCE**

ACCOUNT Tracker

ACCOUNT #1

FINANCIAL INSTITUTION:

ACCOUNT #:

NAME ON ACCOUNT:

ACCOUNT TYPE:

CARD NUMBER:

ROUTING/TRANSIT #:

OTHER:

NOTES

ACCOUNT #2

FINANCIAL INSTITUTION:

ACCOUNT #:

NAME ON ACCOUNT:

ACCOUNT TYPE:

CARD NUMBER:

ROUTING/TRANSIT #:

OTHER:

NOTES

ACCOUNT #3

FINANCIAL INSTITUTION:

ACCOUNT #:

NAME ON ACCOUNT:

ACCOUNT TYPE:

CARD NUMBER:

ROUTING/TRANSIT #:

OTHER:

NOTES

AUTO REPAIR *Tracker*

CAR MAKE: **YEAR:**

CAR MODEL: **VIN #:**

DATE	REPAIR	COST

HOME REPAIR *Tracker*

YEAR:

DATE	REPAIR	COST

MY TRAVEL Budget

BUDGET BREAKDOWN:

PLANE TICKETS**:**

TRANSPORTATION:

LODGING:

FOOD/SHOPPING:

TRAVEL NOTES:

TOTALS:

GOAL PAYOFF DATE

TOTAL COST OF TRIP: AMOUNT TO RAISE:

PAYMENT DATE	**PAYMENT AMOUNT**	**CURRENT BALANCE**

TRAVEL *Contacts*

LOCATION:

HOTEL:

ADDRESS #:

WEBSITE URL:

PHONE#:

AMOUNT PER NIGHT::

RESERVATION INFORMATION: **DUE DATE:**   **ROOM DETAILS:**

BILL TOTAL:

HOTEL:

ACCOUNT #:

WEBSITE URL:

PHONE#:

AMOUNT PER NIGHT::

RESERVATION INFORMATION: **DUE DATE:**   **ROOM DETAILS:**

BILL TOTAL:

HOTEL:

ACCOUNT #:

WEBSITE URL:

PHONE#:

AMOUNT PER NIGHT:

RESERVATION INFORMATION: **DUE DATE:**   **ROOM DETAILS:**

BILL TOTAL:

NOTES

TRAVEL *Contacts*

LOCATION:

CAR RENTAL:

ADDRESS #:   WEBSITE URL:

PHONE#:   AMOUNT PER NIGHT::

RESERVATION INFORMATION: **DUE DATE:**   **CAR DETAILS:**

BILL TOTAL:

CAR RENTAL:

ACCOUNT #:   WEBSITE URL:

PHONE#:   AMOUNT PER NIGHT::

RESERVATION INFORMATION: **DUE DATE:**   **CAR DETAILS:**

BILL TOTAL:

TRAIN PASS:

ACCOUNT #:   WEBSITE URL:

PHONE#:   AMOUNT PER NIGHT:

RESERVATION INFORMATION: **DUE DATE:**   **PASS DETAILS:**

BILL TOTAL:

NOTES

TRAVEL Contacts

LOCATION:

TRAIN PASS:

ADDRESS #: WEBSITE URL:

PHONE#: AMOUNT PER NIGHT::

RESERVATION INFORMATION: **DUE DATE:** **TRAIN DETAILS:**

BILL TOTAL:

AIRPLANE TICKETS:

AIRLINE: WEBSITE URL:

PHONE #: AMOUNT PER SEAT::

RESERVATION INFORMATION: **DUE DATE:** **FLIGHT DETAILS:**

BILL TOTAL:

EVENT TICKETS:

EVENT: WEBSITE URL:

PHONE#: AMOUNT PER TICKET:

RESERVATION INFORMATION: **DUE DATE:** **EVENT DETAILS:**

BILL TOTAL:

NOTES

Planning My Monthly Budget

RECURRING Bills

FREQUENCY:

COMPANY:

ACCOUNT #:   WEBSITE URL:

PHONE#:   BILL DUE DATE:

ONLINE ACCOUNT INFORMATION: **USERNAME**   **PASSWORD**

BILL TOTAL:

COMPANY:

ACCOUNT #:   WEBSITE URL:

PHONE#:   BILL DUE DATE:

ONLINE ACCOUNT INFORMATION: **USERNAME**   **PASSWORD**

BILL TOTAL:

COMPANY:

ACCOUNT #:   WEBSITE URL:

PHONE#:   BILL DUE DATE:

ONLINE ACCOUNT INFORMATION: **USERNAME**   **PASSWORD**

BILL TOTAL:

NOTES

RECURRING *bills*

FREQUENCY:

COMPANY:

ACCOUNT #:   WEBSITE URL:

PHONE #:   BILL DUE DATE:

ONLINE ACCOUNT INFORMATION: **USERNAME**   **PASSWORD**

BILL TOTAL:

COMPANY:

ACCOUNT #:   WEBSITE URL:

PHONE #:   BILL DUE DATE:

ONLINE ACCOUNT INFORMATION: **USERNAME**   **PASSWORD**

BILL TOTAL:

COMPANY:

ACCOUNT #:   WEBSITE URL:

PHONE #:   BILL DUE DATE:

ONLINE ACCOUNT INFORMATION: **USERNAME**   **PASSWORD**

BILL TOTAL:

NOTES

RECURRING *Bills*

FREQUENCY:

COMPANY:

ACCOUNT #:   WEBSITE URL:

PHONE#:   BILL DUE DATE:

ONLINE ACCOUNT INFORMATION: **USERNAME**   **PASSWORD**

BILL TOTAL:

COMPANY:

ACCOUNT #:   WEBSITE URL:

PHONE#:   BILL DUE DATE:

ONLINE ACCOUNT INFORMATION: **USERNAME**   **PASSWORD**

BILL TOTAL:

COMPANY:

ACCOUNT #:   WEBSITE URL:

PHONE#:   BILL DUE DATE:

ONLINE ACCOUNT INFORMATION: **USERNAME**   **PASSWORD**

BILL TOTAL:

NOTES

RECURRING *Bills*

FREQUENCY:

COMPANY:

ACCOUNT #:   WEBSITE URL:

PHONE #:   BILL DUE DATE:

ONLINE ACCOUNT INFORMATION: **USERNAME**   **PASSWORD**

BILL TOTAL:

COMPANY:

ACCOUNT #:   WEBSITE URL:

PHONE #:   BILL DUE DATE:

ONLINE ACCOUNT INFORMATION: **USERNAME**   **PASSWORD**

BILL TOTAL:

COMPANY:

ACCOUNT #:   WEBSITE URL:

PHONE #:   BILL DUE DATE:

ONLINE ACCOUNT INFORMATION: **USERNAME**   **PASSWORD**

BILL TOTAL:

NOTES

INCOME *Tracker*
- MONTHLY -

SOURCE	AMOUNT	M	T	W	T	F	S	S

MONTHLY Budget

MONTHLY INCOME: **BUDGETED:**   **ACTUAL COST:**   **DIFFERENCE:**

Household Utilities/Expenses

SUBTOTAL: **% OF INCOME:**

Debt/Payments/Travel Budget

SUBTOTAL: **% OF INCOME:**

Personal/Other

SUBTOTAL: **% OF INCOME:**

MONTHLY EXPENSE *Tracker*

MONTH:

GROCERIES

DATE	ITEM	AMOUNT

HOME

DATE	ITEM	AMOUNT

PERSONAL

DATE	ITEM	AMOUNT

ACTIVITIES

DATE	ITEM	AMOUNT

RECREATION

DATE	ITEM	AMOUNT

MISC

DATE	ITEM	AMOUNT

Goal Setting & Daily Spending Actuals

MONTH 1

Date:_____

INCOME Tracker
- MONTHLY -

SOURCE	AMOUNT	M	T	W	T	F	S	S

ONE-TIME Bills

MONTH:

COMPANY:

ACCOUNT #:   WEBSITE URL:

PHONE #:   BILL DUE DATE:

ONLINE ACCOUNT INFORMATION: **USERNAME**   **PASSWORD**

BILL TOTAL:

COMPANY:

ACCOUNT #:   WEBSITE URL:

PHONE #:   BILL DUE DATE:

ONLINE ACCOUNT INFORMATION: **USERNAME**   **PASSWORD**

BILL TOTAL:

COMPANY:

ACCOUNT #:   WEBSITE URL:

PHONE #:   BILL DUE DATE:

ONLINE ACCOUNT INFORMATION: **USERNAME**   **PASSWORD**

BILL TOTAL:

NOTES

ONE-TIME Bills

MONTH:

COMPANY:

ACCOUNT #: WEBSITE URL:

PHONE#: BILL DUE DATE:

ONLINE ACCOUNT INFORMATION: **USERNAME** **PASSWORD**

BILL TOTAL:

COMPANY:

ACCOUNT #: WEBSITE URL:

PHONE#: BILL DUE DATE:

ONLINE ACCOUNT INFORMATION: **USERNAME** **PASSWORD**

BILL TOTAL:

COMPANY:

ACCOUNT #: WEBSITE URL:

PHONE#: BILL DUE DATE:

ONLINE ACCOUNT INFORMATION: **USERNAME** **PASSWORD**

BILL TOTAL:

NOTES

WEEKLY EXPENSE *Tracker*

DATES:

DESCRIPTION	CATEGORY	COST	NEED	WANT

DAILY LIFE *Planner*

DATES:

TODAY, *my primary goals are*

MOR

AFT

EVE

TODAY, *my primary goals are*

MOR

AFT

EVE

TODAY, *my primary goals are*

MOR

AFT

EVE

DAILY LIFE *Planner*

DATES:

TODAY, *my primary goals are*

MOR

AFT

EVE

TODAY, *my primary goals are*

MOR

AFT

EVE

TODAY, *my primary goals are*

MOR

AFT

EVE

DAILY LIFE *Planner*

DATES:

TODAY, *my primary goals are*

MOR

AFT

EVE

NOTES:

WEEKLY EXPENSE *Tracker*

DATES:

DESCRIPTION	CATEGORY	COST	NEED	WANT

DAILY LIFE *Planner*

DATES:

TODAY, *my primary goals are*

MOR

AFT

EVE

TODAY, *my primary goals are*

MOR

AFT

EVE

TODAY, *my primary goals are*

MOR

AFT

EVE

DAILY LIFE *Planner*

DATES:

TODAY, *my primary goals are*

MOR　　　　　　　　　　　**AFT**　　　　　　　　　　　**EVE**

TODAY, *my primary goals are*

MOR　　　　　　　　　　　**AFT**　　　　　　　　　　　**EVE**

TODAY, *my primary goals are*

MOR　　　　　　　　　　　**AFT**　　　　　　　　　　　**EVE**

DAILY LIFE *Planner*

DATES:

TODAY, *my primary goals are*

MOR

AFT

EVE

NOTES:

WEEKLY EXPENSE *Tracker*

DATES:

DESCRIPTION	CATEGORY	COST	NEED	WANT

DAILY LIFE *Planner*

DATES:

TODAY, *my primary goals are*

MOR

....
....
....

AFT

....
....
....

EVE

....
....
....

TODAY, *my primary goals are*

MOR

....
....
....

AFT

....
....
....

EVE

....
....
....

TODAY, *my primary goals are*

MOR

....
....
....

AFT

....
....
....

EVE

....
....
....

DAILY LIFE *Planner*

DATES:

TODAY, *my primary goals are*

- MOR
- AFT
- EVE

TODAY, *my primary goals are*

- MOR
- AFT
- EVE

TODAY, *my primary goals are*

- MOR
- AFT
- EVE

DAILY LIFE *Planner*

DATES:

TODAY, *my primary goals are*

MOR

AFT

EVE

NOTES:

WEEKLY EXPENSE *Tracker*

DATES:

DESCRIPTION	CATEGORY	COST	NEED	WANT

DAILY LIFE *Planner*

DATES:

TODAY, *my primary goals are*

MOR

AFT

EVE

TODAY, *my primary goals are*

MOR

AFT

EVE

TODAY, *my primary goals are*

MOR

AFT

EVE

DAILY LIFE *Planner*

DATES:

TODAY, *my primary goals are*

| MOR | AFT | EVE |

TODAY, *my primary goals are*

| MOR | AFT | EVE |

TODAY, *my primary goals are*

| MOR | AFT | EVE |

DAILY LIFE *Planner*

DATES:

TODAY, *my primary goals are*

MOR

AFT

EVE

NOTES:

FINANCIAL *Journal*

MONTH 2

Date:_____

INCOME *Tracker*
- MONTHLY -

SOURCE	AMOUNT	M	T	W	T	F	S	S

ONE-TIME *Bills*

MONTH:

COMPANY:

ACCOUNT #:

WEBSITE URL:

PHONE#:

BILL DUE DATE:

ONLINE ACCOUNT INFORMATION: **USERNAME**   **PASSWORD**

BILL TOTAL:

COMPANY:

ACCOUNT #:

WEBSITE URL:

PHONE#:

BILL DUE DATE:

ONLINE ACCOUNT INFORMATION: **USERNAME**   **PASSWORD**

BILL TOTAL:

COMPANY:

ACCOUNT #:

WEBSITE URL:

PHONE#:

BILL DUE DATE:

ONLINE ACCOUNT INFORMATION: **USERNAME**   **PASSWORD**

BILL TOTAL:

NOTES

ONE-TIME *Bills*

MONTH:

COMPANY:

ACCOUNT #:   WEBSITE URL:

PHONE#:   BILL DUE DATE:

ONLINE ACCOUNT INFORMATION: **USERNAME**   **PASSWORD**

BILL TOTAL:

COMPANY:

ACCOUNT #:   WEBSITE URL:

PHONE#:   BILL DUE DATE:

ONLINE ACCOUNT INFORMATION: **USERNAME**   **PASSWORD**

BILL TOTAL:

COMPANY:

ACCOUNT #:   WEBSITE URL:

PHONE#:   BILL DUE DATE:

ONLINE ACCOUNT INFORMATION: **USERNAME**   **PASSWORD**

BILL TOTAL:

NOTES

WEEKLY EXPENSE *Tracker*

DATES:

DESCRIPTION	CATEGORY	COST	NEED	WANT

DAILY LIFE *Planner*

DATES:

TODAY, *my primary goals are*

MOR

_____
_____
_____
_____

AFT

_____
_____
_____
_____

EVE

_____
_____
_____
_____

TODAY, *my primary goals are*

MOR

_____
_____
_____
_____

AFT

_____
_____
_____
_____

EVE

_____
_____
_____
_____

TODAY, *my primary goals are*

MOR

_____
_____
_____
_____

AFT

_____
_____
_____
_____

EVE

_____
_____
_____
_____

DAILY LIFE *Planner*

DATES:

TODAY, *my primary goals are*

MOR

AFT

EVE

TODAY, *my primary goals are*

MOR

AFT

EVE

TODAY, *my primary goals are*

MOR

AFT

EVE

DAILY LIFE *Planner*

DATES:

TODAY, *my primary goals are*

MOR

AFT

EVE

NOTES:

WEEKLY EXPENSE *Tracker*

DATES:

DESCRIPTION	CATEGORY	COST	NEED	WANT

DAILY LIFE *Planner*

DATES:

TODAY, *my primary goals are*

| MOR | AFT | EVE |

TODAY, *my primary goals are*

| MOR | AFT | EVE |

TODAY, *my primary goals are*

| MOR | AFT | EVE |

DAILY LIFE *Planner*

DATES:

TODAY, *my primary goals are*

MOR

AFT

EVE

TODAY, *my primary goals are*

MOR

AFT

EVE

TODAY, *my primary goals are*

MOR

AFT

EVE

DAILY LIFE *Planner*

DATES:

TODAY, *my primary goals are*

MOR

AFT

EVE

NOTES:

WEEKLY EXPENSE *Tracker*

DATES:

DESCRIPTION	CATEGORY	COST	NEED	WANT

DAILY LIFE *Planner*

DATES:

TODAY, *my primary goals are*

| MOR | AFT | EVE |

TODAY, *my primary goals are*

| MOR | AFT | EVE |

TODAY, *my primary goals are*

| MOR | AFT | EVE |

DAILY LIFE *Planner*

DATES:

TODAY, *my primary goals are*

MOR

AFT

EVE

TODAY, *my primary goals are*

MOR

AFT

EVE

TODAY, *my primary goals are*

MOR

AFT

EVE

DAILY LIFE *Planner*

DATES:

TODAY, *my primary goals are*

MOR

AFT

EVE

NOTES:

WEEKLY EXPENSE *Tracker*

DATES:

DESCRIPTION	CATEGORY	COST	NEED	WANT

DAILY LIFE *Planner*

DATES:

TODAY, *my primary goals are*

| MOR | AFT | EVE |

TODAY, *my primary goals are*

| MOR | AFT | EVE |

TODAY, *my primary goals are*

| MOR | AFT | EVE |

DAILY LIFE *Planner*

DATES:

TODAY, *my primary goals are*

MOR

AFT

EVE

TODAY, *my primary goals are*

MOR

AFT

EVE

TODAY, *my primary goals are*

MOR

AFT

EVE

DAILY LIFE *Planner*

DATES:

TODAY, *my primary goals are*

MOR

AFT

EVE

NOTES:

FINANCIAL Journal

MONTH 3

Date:_____

INCOME *Tracker*
- MONTHLY -

SOURCE	AMOUNT	M	T	W	T	F	S	S

ONE-TIME Bills

MONTH:

COMPANY:

ACCOUNT #:   WEBSITE URL:

PHONE #:   BILL DUE DATE:

ONLINE ACCOUNT INFORMATION: **USERNAME**   **PASSWORD**

BILL TOTAL:

COMPANY:

ACCOUNT #:   WEBSITE URL:

PHONE #:   BILL DUE DATE:

ONLINE ACCOUNT INFORMATION: **USERNAME**   **PASSWORD**

BILL TOTAL:

COMPANY:

ACCOUNT #:   WEBSITE URL:

PHONE #:   BILL DUE DATE:

ONLINE ACCOUNT INFORMATION: **USERNAME**   **PASSWORD**

BILL TOTAL:

NOTES

ONE-TIME Bills

MONTH:

COMPANY:

ACCOUNT #:   WEBSITE URL:

PHONE#:   BILL DUE DATE:

ONLINE ACCOUNT INFORMATION: **USERNAME**   **PASSWORD**

BILL TOTAL:

COMPANY:

ACCOUNT #:   WEBSITE URL:

PHONE#:   BILL DUE DATE:

ONLINE ACCOUNT INFORMATION: **USERNAME**   **PASSWORD**

BILL TOTAL:

COMPANY:

ACCOUNT #:   WEBSITE URL:

PHONE#:   BILL DUE DATE:

ONLINE ACCOUNT INFORMATION: **USERNAME**   **PASSWORD**

BILL TOTAL:

NOTES

WEEKLY EXPENSE *Tracker*

DATES:

DESCRIPTION	CATEGORY	COST	NEED	WANT

DAILY LIFE *Planner*

DATES:

TODAY, *my primary goals are*

- MOR
- AFT
- EVE

TODAY, *my primary goals are*

- MOR
- AFT
- EVE

TODAY, *my primary goals are*

- MOR
- AFT
- EVE

DAILY LIFE *Planner*

DATES:

TODAY, *my primary goals are*

- **MOR**
- **AFT**
- **EVE**

TODAY, *my primary goals are*

- **MOR**
- **AFT**
- **EVE**

TODAY, *my primary goals are*

- **MOR**
- **AFT**
- **EVE**

DAILY LIFE *Planner*

DATES:

TODAY, *my primary goals are*

MOR

AFT

EVE

NOTES:

WEEKLY EXPENSE *Tracker*

DATES:

DESCRIPTION	CATEGORY	COST	NEED	WANT

DAILY LIFE *Planner*

DATES:

TODAY, *my primary goals are*

MOR	AFT	EVE

TODAY, *my primary goals are*

MOR	AFT	EVE

TODAY, *my primary goals are*

MOR	AFT	EVE

DAILY LIFE *Planner*

DATES:

TODAY, *my primary goals are*

| MOR | AFT | EVE |

_____

TODAY, *my primary goals are*

| MOR | AFT | EVE |

_____

TODAY, *my primary goals are*

| MOR | AFT | EVE |

DAILY LIFE *Planner*

DATES:

TODAY, *my primary goals are*

MOR

AFT

EVE

NOTES:

WEEKLY EXPENSE *Tracker*

DATES:

DESCRIPTION	CATEGORY	COST	NEED	WANT

DAILY LIFE *Planner*

DATES:

TODAY, *my primary goals are*

MOR

AFT

EVE

TODAY, *my primary goals are*

MOR

AFT

EVE

TODAY, *my primary goals are*

MOR

AFT

EVE

DAILY LIFE *Planner*

DATES:

TODAY, *my primary goals are*

| MOR | AFT | EVE |

TODAY, *my primary goals are*

| MOR | AFT | EVE |

TODAY, *my primary goals are*

| MOR | AFT | EVE |

DAILY LIFE *Planner*

DATES:

TODAY, *my primary goals are*

MOR

AFT

EVE

NOTES:

WEEKLY EXPENSE *Tracker*

DATES:

DESCRIPTION	CATEGORY	COST	NEED	WANT

DAILY LIFE *Planner*

DATES:

TODAY, *my primary goals are*

MOR

AFT

EVE

TODAY, *my primary goals are*

MOR

AFT

EVE

TODAY, *my primary goals are*

MOR

AFT

EVE

DAILY LIFE *Planner*

DATES:

TODAY, *my primary goals are*

MOR
_____
_____
_____
_____

AFT
_____
_____
_____
_____

EVE
_____
_____
_____
_____

TODAY, *my primary goals are*

MOR
_____
_____
_____
_____

AFT
_____
_____
_____
_____

EVE
_____
_____
_____
_____

TODAY, *my primary goals are*

MOR
_____
_____
_____
_____

AFT
_____
_____
_____
_____

EVE
_____
_____
_____
_____

DAILY LIFE *Planner*

DATES:

TODAY, *my primary goals are*

MOR

AFT

EVE

NOTES:

FINANCIAL *Journal*

MONTH 4

Date:_____

INCOME *Tracker*
- MONTHLY -

SOURCE	AMOUNT	M	T	W	T	F	S	S

ONE-TIME Bills

MONTH:

COMPANY:

ACCOUNT #:   WEBSITE URL:

PHONE#:   BILL DUE DATE:

ONLINE ACCOUNT INFORMATION: **USERNAME**   **PASSWORD**

BILL TOTAL:

COMPANY:

ACCOUNT #:   WEBSITE URL:

PHONE#:   BILL DUE DATE:

ONLINE ACCOUNT INFORMATION: **USERNAME**   **PASSWORD**

BILL TOTAL:

COMPANY:

ACCOUNT #:   WEBSITE URL:

PHONE#:   BILL DUE DATE:

ONLINE ACCOUNT INFORMATION: **USERNAME**   **PASSWORD**

BILL TOTAL:

NOTES

ONE-TIME Bills

MONTH:

COMPANY:

ACCOUNT #:　　　　　　　　　　　　　　　WEBSITE URL:

PHONE#:　　　　　　　　　　　　　　　　　BILL DUE DATE:

ONLINE ACCOUNT INFORMATION:　　　　**USERNAME**　　　**PASSWORD**

BILL TOTAL:

COMPANY:

ACCOUNT #:　　　　　　　　　　　　　　　WEBSITE URL:

PHONE#:　　　　　　　　　　　　　　　　　BILL DUE DATE:

ONLINE ACCOUNT INFORMATION:　　　　**USERNAME**　　　**PASSWORD**

BILL TOTAL:

COMPANY:

ACCOUNT #:　　　　　　　　　　　　　　　WEBSITE URL:

PHONE#:　　　　　　　　　　　　　　　　　BILL DUE DATE:

ONLINE ACCOUNT INFORMATION:　　　　**USERNAME**　　　**PASSWORD**

BILL TOTAL:

NOTES

WEEKLY EXPENSE *Tracker*

DATES:

DESCRIPTION	CATEGORY	COST	NEED	WANT

DAILY LIFE *Planner*

DATES:

TODAY, *my primary goals are*

| MOR | AFT | EVE |

TODAY, *my primary goals are*

| MOR | AFT | EVE |

TODAY, *my primary goals are*

| MOR | AFT | EVE |

DAILY LIFE *Planner*

DATES:

TODAY, *my primary goals are*

MOR

AFT

EVE

TODAY, *my primary goals are*

MOR

AFT

EVE

TODAY, *my primary goals are*

MOR

AFT

EVE

DAILY LIFE *Planner*

DATES:

TODAY, *my primary goals are*

MOR

AFT

EVE

NOTES:

WEEKLY EXPENSE *Tracker*

DATES:

DESCRIPTION	CATEGORY	COST	NEED	WANT

DAILY LIFE *Planner*

DATES:

TODAY, *my primary goals are*

MOR
_____
_____
_____

AFT
_____
_____
_____

EVE
_____
_____
_____

TODAY, *my primary goals are*

MOR
_____
_____
_____

AFT
_____
_____
_____

EVE
_____
_____
_____

TODAY, *my primary goals are*

MOR
_____
_____
_____

AFT
_____
_____
_____

EVE
_____
_____
_____

DAILY LIFE *Planner*

DATES:

TODAY, *my primary goals are*

MOR	AFT	EVE

TODAY, *my primary goals are*

MOR	AFT	EVE

TODAY, *my primary goals are*

MOR	AFT	EVE

DAILY LIFE *Planner*

DATES:

TODAY, *my primary goals are*

MOR

AFT

EVE

NOTES:

WEEKLY EXPENSE *Tracker*

DATES:

DESCRIPTION	CATEGORY	COST	NEED	WANT

DAILY LIFE *Planner*

DATES:

TODAY, *my primary goals are*

MOR

AFT

EVE

TODAY, *my primary goals are*

MOR

AFT

EVE

TODAY, *my primary goals are*

MOR

AFT

EVE

DAILY LIFE *Planner*

DATES:

TODAY, *my primary goals are*

MOR

AFT

EVE

TODAY, *my primary goals are*

MOR

AFT

EVE

TODAY, *my primary goals are*

MOR

AFT

EVE

DAILY LIFE *Planner*

DATES:

TODAY, *my primary goals are*

MOR

AFT

EVE

NOTES:

WEEKLY EXPENSE *Tracker*

DATES:

DESCRIPTION	CATEGORY	COST	NEED	WANT

DAILY LIFE *Planner*

DATES:

TODAY, *my primary goals are*

| MOR | AFT | EVE |

TODAY, *my primary goals are*

| MOR | AFT | EVE |

TODAY, *my primary goals are*

| MOR | AFT | EVE |

DAILY LIFE Planner

DATES:

TODAY, *my primary goals are*

MOR

AFT

EVE

TODAY, *my primary goals are*

MOR

AFT

EVE

TODAY, *my primary goals are*

MOR

AFT

EVE

DAILY LIFE *Planner*

DATES:

TODAY, *my primary goals are*

MOR

AFT

EVE

NOTES:

FINANCIAL Journal

MONTH 5

Date:_____

INCOME *Tracker*
- MONTHLY -

SOURCE	AMOUNT	M	T	W	T	F	S	S

ONE-TIME Bills

MONTH:

COMPANY:

ACCOUNT #:   WEBSITE URL:

PHONE#:   BILL DUE DATE:

ONLINE ACCOUNT INFORMATION: **USERNAME**   **PASSWORD**

BILL TOTAL:

COMPANY:

ACCOUNT #:   WEBSITE URL:

PHONE#:   BILL DUE DATE:

ONLINE ACCOUNT INFORMATION: **USERNAME**   **PASSWORD**

BILL TOTAL:

COMPANY:

ACCOUNT #:   WEBSITE URL:

PHONE#:   BILL DUE DATE:

ONLINE ACCOUNT INFORMATION: **USERNAME**   **PASSWORD**

BILL TOTAL:

NOTES

ONE-TIME Bills

MONTH:

COMPANY:

ACCOUNT #: WEBSITE URL:

PHONE#: BILL DUE DATE:

ONLINE ACCOUNT INFORMATION: **USERNAME** **PASSWORD**

BILL TOTAL:

COMPANY:

ACCOUNT #: WEBSITE URL:

PHONE#: BILL DUE DATE:

ONLINE ACCOUNT INFORMATION: **USERNAME** **PASSWORD**

BILL TOTAL:

COMPANY:

ACCOUNT #: WEBSITE URL:

PHONE#: BILL DUE DATE:

ONLINE ACCOUNT INFORMATION: **USERNAME** **PASSWORD**

BILL TOTAL:

NOTES

WEEKLY EXPENSE *Tracker*

DATES:

DESCRIPTION	CATEGORY	COST	NEED	WANT

DAILY LIFE *Planner*

DATES:

TODAY, *my primary goals are*

MOR

AFT

EVE

TODAY, *my primary goals are*

MOR

AFT

EVE

TODAY, *my primary goals are*

MOR

AFT

EVE

DAILY LIFE *Planner*

DATES:

TODAY, *my primary goals are*

MOR

AFT

EVE

TODAY, *my primary goals are*

MOR

AFT

EVE

TODAY, *my primary goals are*

MOR

AFT

EVE

DAILY LIFE *Planner*

DATES:

TODAY, *my primary goals are*

MOR

AFT

EVE

NOTES:

WEEKLY EXPENSE *Tracker*

DATES:

DESCRIPTION	CATEGORY	COST	NEED	WANT

DAILY LIFE *Planner*

DATES:

TODAY, *my primary goals are*

MOR

AFT

EVE

TODAY, *my primary goals are*

MOR

AFT

EVE

TODAY, *my primary goals are*

MOR

AFT

EVE

DAILY LIFE *Planner*

DATES:

TODAY, *my primary goals are*

MOR

AFT

EVE

TODAY, *my primary goals are*

MOR

AFT

EVE

TODAY, *my primary goals are*

MOR

AFT

EVE

DAILY LIFE *Planner*

DATES:

TODAY, *my primary goals are*

MOR

AFT

EVE

NOTES:

WEEKLY EXPENSE *Tracker*

DATES:

DESCRIPTION	CATEGORY	COST	NEED	WANT

DAILY LIFE *Planner*

DATES:

TODAY, *my primary goals are*

MOR

AFT

EVE

TODAY, *my primary goals are*

MOR

AFT

EVE

TODAY, *my primary goals are*

MOR

AFT

EVE

DAILY LIFE *Planner*

DATES:

TODAY, *my primary goals are*

MOR

AFT

EVE

TODAY, *my primary goals are*

MOR

AFT

EVE

TODAY, *my primary goals are*

MOR

AFT

EVE

DAILY LIFE *Planner*

DATES:

TODAY, *my primary goals are*

MOR

AFT

EVE

NOTES:

WEEKLY EXPENSE *Tracker*

DATES:

DESCRIPTION	CATEGORY	COST	NEED	WANT

DAILY LIFE *Planner*

DATES:

TODAY, *my primary goals are*

MOR

AFT

EVE

TODAY, *my primary goals are*

MOR

AFT

EVE

TODAY, *my primary goals are*

MOR

AFT

EVE

DAILY LIFE *Planner*

DATES:

TODAY, *my primary goals are*

| MOR | AFT | EVE |

TODAY, *my primary goals are*

| MOR | AFT | EVE |

TODAY, *my primary goals are*

| MOR | AFT | EVE |

DAILY LIFE *Planner*

DATES:

TODAY, *my primary goals are*

MOR

AFT

EVE

NOTES:

FINANCIAL *Journal*

MONTH 6

Date:_____

INCOME Tracker
- MONTHLY -

SOURCE	AMOUNT	M	T	W	T	F	S	S

ONE-TIME Bills

MONTH:

COMPANY:

ACCOUNT #:

PHONE#:

WEBSITE URL:

BILL DUE DATE:

ONLINE ACCOUNT INFORMATION: **USERNAME** **PASSWORD**

BILL TOTAL:

COMPANY:

ACCOUNT #:

PHONE#:

WEBSITE URL:

BILL DUE DATE:

ONLINE ACCOUNT INFORMATION: **USERNAME** **PASSWORD**

BILL TOTAL:

COMPANY:

ACCOUNT #:

PHONE#:

WEBSITE URL:

BILL DUE DATE:

ONLINE ACCOUNT INFORMATION: **USERNAME** **PASSWORD**

BILL TOTAL:

NOTES

ONE-TIME *Bills*

MONTH:

COMPANY:

ACCOUNT #:   WEBSITE URL:

PHONE#:   BILL DUE DATE:

ONLINE ACCOUNT INFORMATION: **USERNAME**   **PASSWORD**

BILL TOTAL:

COMPANY:

ACCOUNT #:   WEBSITE URL:

PHONE#:   BILL DUE DATE:

ONLINE ACCOUNT INFORMATION: **USERNAME**   **PASSWORD**

BILL TOTAL:

COMPANY:

ACCOUNT #:   WEBSITE URL:

PHONE#:   BILL DUE DATE:

ONLINE ACCOUNT INFORMATION: **USERNAME**   **PASSWORD**

BILL TOTAL:

NOTES

WEEKLY EXPENSE *Tracker*

DATES:

DESCRIPTION	CATEGORY	COST	NEED	WANT

DAILY LIFE *Planner*

DATES:

TODAY, *my primary goals are*

MOR
....
....
....
....

AFT
....
....
....
....

EVE
....
....
....
....

TODAY, *my primary goals are*

MOR
....
....
....
....

AFT
....
....
....
....

EVE
....
....
....
....

TODAY, *my primary goals are*

MOR
....
....
....
....

AFT
....
....
....
....

EVE
....
....
....
....

DAILY LIFE *Planner*

DATES:

TODAY, *my primary goals are*

MOR	AFT	EVE

TODAY, *my primary goals are*

MOR	AFT	EVE

TODAY, *my primary goals are*

MOR	AFT	EVE

DAILY LIFE *Planner*

DATES:

TODAY, *my primary goals are*

MOR

AFT

EVE

NOTES:

WEEKLY EXPENSE Tracker

DATES:

DESCRIPTION	CATEGORY	COST	NEED	WANT

DAILY LIFE *Planner*

DATES:

TODAY, *my primary goals are*

MOR

AFT

EVE

TODAY, *my primary goals are*

MOR

AFT

EVE

TODAY, *my primary goals are*

MOR

AFT

EVE

DAILY LIFE *Planner*

DATES:

TODAY, *my primary goals are*

MOR

AFT

EVE

TODAY, *my primary goals are*

MOR

AFT

EVE

TODAY, *my primary goals are*

MOR

AFT

EVE

DAILY LIFE *Planner*

DATES:

TODAY, *my primary goals are*

MOR

AFT

EVE

NOTES:

WEEKLY EXPENSE *Tracker*

DATES:

DESCRIPTION	CATEGORY	COST	NEED	WANT

DAILY LIFE *Planner*

DATES:

TODAY, *my primary goals are*

MOR

_____
_____
_____
_____

AFT

_____
_____
_____
_____

EVE

_____
_____
_____
_____

TODAY, *my primary goals are*

MOR

_____
_____
_____
_____

AFT

_____
_____
_____
_____

EVE

_____
_____
_____
_____

TODAY, *my primary goals are*

MOR

_____
_____
_____
_____

AFT

_____
_____
_____
_____

EVE

_____
_____
_____
_____

DAILY LIFE *Planner*

DATES:

TODAY, *my primary goals are*

| MOR | AFT | EVE |

TODAY, *my primary goals are*

| MOR | AFT | EVE |

TODAY, *my primary goals are*

| MOR | AFT | EVE |

DAILY LIFE *Planner*

DATES:

TODAY, *my primary goals are*

MOR

AFT

EVE

NOTES:

WEEKLY EXPENSE *Tracker*

DATES:

DESCRIPTION	CATEGORY	COST	NEED	WANT

DAILY LIFE *Planner*

DATES:

TODAY, *my primary goals are*

MOR

AFT

EVE

TODAY, *my primary goals are*

MOR

AFT

EVE

TODAY, *my primary goals are*

MOR

AFT

EVE

DAILY LIFE *Planner*

DATES:

TODAY, *my primary goals are*

MOR	AFT	EVE

TODAY, *my primary goals are*

MOR	AFT	EVE

TODAY, *my primary goals are*

MOR	AFT	EVE

DAILY LIFE *Planner*

DATES:

TODAY, *my primary goals are*

MOR

AFT

EVE

NOTES:

FINANCIAL Journal

Made in the USA
Middletown, DE
02 October 2022